soft eyes and troubled minds
LITERARY WORKS FOR THE DISTURBED AT HEART

by E.S.P. & I.C.L.

This novel is a work of fiction. Any resemblances to real people, living or dead, actual events, establishments, organizations, locales are intended to give the fiction a sense of reality and authenticity. Other names, characters, places and incidents are either products of the author's imagination or are used fictitiously.

Written By E.S.P. and I.C.L.
Copyright 2016 Mind Candy, LLC.
ISBN 10: 0-692-68425-5
ISBN 13: 978-0-692-68425-2

Written by E.S.P. and I.C.L. for Mind Candy, LLC.
Edited by E.S.P.

Cover illustration by Moriah G. Morales Lopez
Authors' photo by Elijah Carrasco

Printed in the United States

Published by:

Mind Candy, LLC.
P.O. Box 2185
Garden City, NY 11531-2185
info@MindCandyMedia.com

Dedicated To:

All the people who have ended or almost ended their lives. You do not have to go through this alone.
~I.C.L.

My parents. Sorry about this.

And to everyone currently dealing with body image issues. Honestly, I think you look gorgeous.
~E.S.P.

table of contents

A Note from the Authors

The small amount of time we've spent on this earth has been filled with experiences, emotions, and memories that have shaped us into who we are. We hide the bad ones and parade the good ones, never letting anyone forget that something good did come out of this life once. Why do we do that? Why are people so afraid to admit they're not happy all the time?

It's time to start taking the good with the bad. There is beauty to be found in pain. Without rain, there can be no growth. Without struggle, you cannot recognize success.

Soft Eyes and Troubled Minds is everything you've been afraid to say, every feeling you could never put into words. Here is where you discover that you're not alone, and you never have to be again.

The world is a dark and dangerous place. Let us clear your mind.

soft eyes

Soft eyes
that melt stone
A smile that makes the Sun
Look like a candle,
Three miles away.
A personality
that can bring you back from The Pit.
And she chose me.
But
she can't say the three words I want to hear.
And that's okay.
We don't have that much time,
before she disappears.
I don't know if she'll come back
or if she'll choose me again
And that's a fate worse than hell.
But I will always love those soft eyes
and hope that she will be as happy
as I am with her.
~I.C.L.

school blues :(

Well dressed in a gray polo with matching shoes
Six AM alarm singing the old school blues
Goodbye to the sweet life of summer livin'
Hello to my nine-month stay in scholastic prison

Walking in, all the inmates give me a look
Everyone was lighter in the yearbook
Exotic stories are shared before the bell
Thrust back into routine like a witch's spell

Ten minutes in and we're already trying too hard
We're wearing our personas with our egos at guard
Its second period and my brain is already tired
Shoulda hit snooze or just retired

With school as my muse I'm uninspired
Cafeteria gossip I have no desire
I'm alone amid drones like every year
I'm a deer stuck in headlights, paralyzed with fear

But why dwell on that when it's the end of the day
My peers might think I'm weird or even gay
In time I'm bound to conform and get back on track
Here comes the school blues. It's good to be back.
                    ~E.S.P.

how to make a summer romance

First find your loved ones. Keep them close.
Add fun times.
Sprinkle laughter and fun stories.
Mix with embarrassing moments and watermelon.
Add a friend you can be happy with,
Someone you can talk with for hours.
Treasure them.
Add long walks
Holding hands,
Children chanting K-I-S-S-I-N-G,
And falling asleep together.
Bake for an entire summer at the heat of your passion.
Once it is done let it cool,
And remember how fun it was.
~I.C.L.

on wednesdays we

We're hot we're vile we're vicious we're mean
You see us on your TV screen
We play hard to get, we get you hard
Our faces are our Mastercards!

You envy us, you stare us down
You want our title, you crave our crown
We don't care, we're totally cool
Our outfits slay, our style rules!

We're always in, we're the new black
You wanna buy us drinks, you like our racks
You give us your number, but we'll never call
We rule the school, we own the mall!

We're catty we're petty we're flaky we're fake
We're always there, you'll never escape
You can try to hide, you can attempt to run
But there's a mean girl for everyone!
~E.S.P.

rumors

Don't tell anyone but Ashley and I just did it.
OMG I won't tell I promise.
Hey, did you hear about Ashley?
Yeah, I heard her and Dylan had sex!
Really? No way! I heard it was just oral.
Listen to this: Ashley had sex with Dylan. I heard they didn't wear a
rubber.
Hey guys, I just heard Ashley's pregnant.
Dude I heard Ashley's pregnant and whoring around.
Hey Cat, did you hear that Ashley did it with five guys last week?
Isn't she pregnant?
Hey, look it's the pregnant thot!
Lol!
OMG!
Lmfao!
Hey guys did you hear about Ashley?
Yeah...she's the pregnant thot.
No dude...she killed herself.
OMG no way.
Yeah. Forreal.
But...did you hear about Mary and Todd?
~I.C.L.

karma

I'm hot, you're not
I'm the flame that burns the pot
The stain on your favorite top
The plague that ruins the crops
I'm style, I'm jest
I declined your AmEx
Hey, maybe I even caused that awful car wreck

So don't blame it on spirits, don't blame it on hex
Better look out girl because you might be next
Look out girl 'cause you might be next.
Look out girl 'cause you might be next.

They call me mean, green
But I'm somewhere in between
I'm hate, irate
Skates to your figure eight
It's demonic, ironic
Creepy and chaotic
So don't say bye to your sin, 'cause it'll be back
'Cause I'm tat for tit, tit for tat

So don't blame it on spirits, don't blame it on hex
Better look out girl because you might be next
Look out girl 'cause you might be next.
Look out girl 'cause you might be next.

I'm not cold, nor warm
I take on any form
I'm the burglar that robbed your college dorm
I'm not kind, nor nice
I give you bad advice
'Cause every sin comes with a price

Hate to say it, didn't want to alarm her
But nice to meet you my name is Karma.
Nice to meet you, my name is Karma.
Nice to meet you, my name is Karma.
~E.S.P.

quack

Sanity is the humdrum Quack
of a duck floating in the pond.
A woman walking down the street.
A man typing his dull email to
a person he's never met.
It's the following of society
as a mindless drone.

Insanity is the Quack of
a talking cow walking on stardust.
It is the woman licking a lollipop street
with cupcake sprinkles.
It is a man riding a watermelon
into an Oreo pool.
It is the rainbow of the universe.
It is what you know society wants
and you bend over, show it a full moon
and fly away to create your own Quacking path.
~I.C.L

the wicked games

Greetings all! We're glad you came
To join us for our annual Wicked Games!
We break hearts like nails just for sport
Have tissues ready! We need support!

First, we have the lovely Reese Bell
Who thinks his relationship is going swell!
Too bad his girl gave it up for two packs and a joint
And bed his best friend for ten extra points!

This next heartbreaker is young and on the rise
He is aiming for our combo prize!
Him and his girl were great. They had their own song!
Until he dropped when she said she was two weeks along!

Our last one is the real kicker
On the back of her van is a "safe sex" sticker!
She has a hundred points up for grabs
Because she infected six with genital crabs!

This year's Wicked Games rose to expectation
And frankly, that deserves a celebration!
So c'mon! Break a heart over a five star dinner
Because in the game of love, we're all winners!
~E.S.P.

wedding day jitters

Well you've definitely ruined my day
By promising you loved me
And leaving me at the alter
As my family,
And your family,
Stared at me in pity
I looked out the window,
Why, I do not know.
Maybe, to find God,
Or wonder where you've gone,
But out that window I saw
A clown
Picking his nose.
It looked like he was digging for gold.
He wriggled and wrangled and spun
When he found his treasure
He rubbed it on his pants
And walked away in a limousine.
As he drove away I wondered
Where is he going in our limousine?
~I.C.L.

vigil

The age old quilt
tells of the carnival
and its shadows.
The wafting of the smell of milkshakes
with their curdled milk.
The blossoming flower
with its poisonous thorns.
It tells of the opaque bell
its beautiful sounds
and the slave that rings it.
The fireside vigil
and the death of the children.
~I.C.L.

this was supposed to be a positive poem

I wanna run, travel to the ends of the earth with you
Where the snow is untouched and adventures are new
But my heart is failing and baby I'm in pain
And I've got nothing but this sick, sad world to blame

This power, social status, acceptance we chase
You see it as life but I think life's a waste
You follow the crowd, I travel by sea
I said join me chasing the clouds, you trampled over me

I was your shoulder to cry on when nobody cared
I was your cliff to dive off when nobody dared
You were my broken parachute a hundred meters from the ground
You only addressed me by baby when there was no one around

You gave me reality when I wanted to dream
You gave me space when I needed a team
You're an addiction, one I need to shake
But withdrawal is more than my heart can take

So if we ran it'd be to an earthly hell
Knowing you, you'd like that and I know you well
I know I'm sick, baby, but you're a corpse
Yet I keep coming back so which is worse?

I wanna run, travel to the ends of the world with you
Leave my skin untouched 'cause I'm feeling blue
Come and join me under this starfilled sky
Where no one's around to hear me cry
~E.S.P.

blind people

We talk,
we laugh,
we joke,
we play.
I see it
the connection.
The spark in her eyes
The way she touches my arms
I can feel the smile jump on my face
When she calls me her friend,
and my heart
explodes.
Maybe I was blind,
too blind to see her.
To see past her eyes,
face,
body,
personality,
and into her heart.
But how could she not see mine?
Maybe she's blind too.
~I.C.L.

this small town

She's got an hour to commit eighty vocab words to memory
She's taking physics now but recalls the chemistry
True, she got some damn good poems out the bind
And having books on her mind is all she got time for

Up at five AM, in bed past ten
Wakes up the next day and does it again
Crazy how much a difference having goals can make
She's thinks she made a mistake 'cause her friends call her "The Fake
One"

She's loves the people, the vibes, the weather
But she can't be repping this small town forever

Her heart's in the Hamptons, here's where she resides
Work at six so she can get out the North side
When she has time she thinks about her dreams
She goes to extremes for her dreams at least that's what it seems like

She wants to chill and be a kid but she got goals
Tired in part, determined as a whole
Working so hard, too busy to chase the crowd
Making her family proud, that's all she's about now

She loves the people, the vibes, the weather
But she can't be repping this small town forever
~E.S.P.

when?

When?
When does the time for fun start?
They say later.
I've been waiting.
I've done my work,
Gotten great grades,
Done homework till the birds chirped.
Sleep is my mistress.
My friends go out to party,
To have fun.
I do my work.
What's the point of having a great future?
If you never got to enjoy yourself.
The greatest tragedy
Is the waste of youth.
~I.C.L.

numb

Stare into the ocean deep
Listen to hear the Syrians weep
Dip in one toe just for show
To ensure the crowd is here for keeps

Lean in too far and you might drown
And if you choke, who will be around?
Don't taste to savor if you're not a savior
You're only choice is to risk sinking down

Come on, you're the boldest of the bold
For a rebel you sure do what you're told
You thought you could lose commotion in the ocean
Until your heart felt the cold
~E.S.P.

mask

I am a jester.
At least that's what my mask says.
I make jokes,
I smile,
I am happy.
At least that's what my mask does.
People only see the mask.
They don't see what's under it.
It's just a black teenager that
is never truly happy.
That wants someone who he can tell anything to, even
his secrets.
Someone he can take his mask off for.
Someone who after seeing the man under the mask
won't run in terror.
Someone he can trust
and love
without being hurt.
Can someone please take off my mask?

Please?
~I.C.L.

barbie

When I was a little girl I got my first doll
Little bleach blond Barbie was the fairest of them all
I would dress her nice and decorate the house to please Ken
Then replay the day to do it again

Barbie could be anything. A cook, just not a chef.
A housewife who could separate a man's right socks from his left
A dancer, a movie star, not a doctor, but a nurse
A fashion designer with glitter on her pink purse

Why Barbie could be anything she imagined. Well that is,
If it didn't interrupt her caring for her husband and kids
She could learn the world's secrets and be whomever she wished
As long as the house was clean and dinner was ready by six

Young girls are cultured since their birth
That a wife and a mother is the limit of their worth
Their first toy a baby doll, they are taught to nurture and care
So they can grow up like Barbie with her bleach blond hair

The sky's the limit, as long as it's not far from the kitchen
As long as your work ethic isn't swallowed by ambition
Just make sure you dress nice and please dear Ken
Then replay the day and do it again.
~E.S.P.

car accident

If you've ever been in a car accident
there is something interesting that happens.
Everything stops before the car hits you.
I always feel like I was in a car accident
when I get my heart broken.
Because that moment before
she speaks the words that'll poison my mind
everything stops.
And the world takes a deep breath.
In that moment I like to pray.
Pray that she doesn't speak the words I know she'll say.
It's not my fault apparently,
it never is,
but then who's is it?
Now I'm just waiting
for this car to hit me,
and hope,
that this time will be my last.
~I.C.L.

daddy's girl

Tell me father, what does "daddy's girl" mean?
Does it mean I'm beautiful? That I'm a queen?
Would you still whisper, "I love you" to me each night
If I walked on the left instead of the right?

Would you hold me close and give me a kiss
If you knew you weren't the only one to touch my lips?
Would you still promise me the world if you knew
Someone else made the same promise to me too?

When you said your love was unconditional, was that a lie?
Like when you called me the apple of your eye?
Because now that I'm not the queen you once knew
I wonder if your love was ever true

Tell me father, do you know what "daddy's girl" means?
Am I still beautiful? Am I still a queen?
Would you still think I'm the fairest one around
If you knew I left the throne without my crown?
~E.S.P.

where am I?

I have fallen into the void.
Only you can save me.
If only you would notice me.

I have fallen into the void.
Its darkness enfolds me.
If only you would notice me.
Let me out of here.

Its darkness enfolds me.
You could be my shining light.
Let me out of here.
Please.

You could be my shining light.
Only you can save me.
Please.
Where am I?
~I.C.L.

⅙ *of a minute*

Take a deep breath, count to ten, they say
In just a sixth of a minute all your troubles will go away
There is a rainbow after every grey sky
Despite your tears, pain, and heartache kiss your anger goodbye

Ten seconds later and I am not subsiding
Living in a world where we do less seeking than hiding
An emotion that's not happiness must not be seen
Gone in ten seconds before it finds its mean

In just ten seconds all my troubles are veiled
Masked by fantastic happiness in an abundance of scales
As to not make anyone uncomfortable, they say
So I mute dim reality and put on a display

Just an ounce of simple daily frustration
Perceived as a narcissistic lack of appreciation
When you fortunate to be as privileged as me
It is a crime to not be bursting with glee

If those ten seconds were surpassed, what would the world become?
Would it explode into hell if we ever knew one?
Or would a sliver of humanity finally manage to come through
As we address these foreign emotions that we never knew?

As the countdown draws near I take a deep breath
Willing God to double the ounce of patience I have left
One sixth of a minute and all my troubles end
And happiness arrives in 8...9...10.
~E.S.P.

i can't take it anymore

I can't take it anymore
Every day
Every second
There is something to do.
Then it starts piling up.
Piling up quicker than I can complete them.
It starts surrounding me
Until I can't breathe.
Will I ever be at peace?
Will I ever have a moment's rest?
Just to gather myself?
To fix the shell of a person I once was?
Buried beneath the smile
The laughter
Is stress,
Worry,
Pride,
Desperation,
Loneliness.
They don't care.
None of these so-called educators care
They just put more on the pile.
Deadlines intersect.
Sports, music, school.
I can't have one without the other two.
Yet, I can't handle all three.
There is only one of me.
I wonder how quick it would be
To pull the trigger.
~I.C.L.

just tired.

"I'm tired," is the excuse I give for my behavior.
The defeat you see in my eyes.
Really, I'm thinking about a text sent months ago
And what I wish I said instead

Nights are hard because I'm all alone
My mind stares itself in the mirror, my soul searches for sleep
I vandalize the memories under your name
I wake up empty and sleep full of pain

"I'm tired" will never be the reason why
I'm a liar as long as I answer that way
I smile and ask "How was your weekend?"
And pull off the facade flawlessly again

It's all too simple really
A smile here, a laugh or two
You notice something different
But in time you will forget to care
~E.S.P.

puff puff pass

What is love?
Why don't she love me?
Puff.
It's because you're depressing.
Pass.
Puff.
It's because you love her too much;
you might be freaking her out.
Puff.
She's a weird girl.
Pass. Puff.
Not weird. Unique.
She's one of a kind.
And I fell for her really, really hard.
Puff.
Pass.
Puff puff puff
Bro, chill you're gonna kill it.
I can't love a person who doesn't love me.
I just wanna stay high
and never fall again.
~I.C.L.

doppelgänger

Someday I'll meet the other version of me
The me who took her own advice
We'll both be smiling but hers will be convincing
Like she's happy right where she is

There will be this glow to her
No amount of makeup could replicate
And I'll just be standing there wondering
How she gets the sun to follow her like that

Somewhere there's another version of me
Wondering where'd she be if she hadn't been so smart
Wondering just how horrible her life could be
I'll let her know when I see her.
~E.S.P.

rough draft

I must be a rough draft.
A better person will be made from my mistakes.
He will be stronger and better than me.
People will like him more.
He will stand triumphant over my mistakes.
All I am is a stepping-stone for his greatness.
I must be a rough draft
And the rough draft is always thrown out.
~I.C.L.

PLAYMATE

Those poor, poor single days
Filled with mixed emotions and desperate haze
Delusional desire, obsession and fawning
Causing sleepless nights and morning yawning

She wanted love, kindness, and affection
All he had was marijuana and an erection
Her desperation to love was met with passionless hugs
And piss colored beer stains on her bedroom rug

He wanted a playmate for all day and night
That would keep him satisfied without a fight
Instead he got a creature with emotion and depth
With her own desires that would never be met

Love is not obtainable for it is simply a dream
That causes not swooning, but the need to scream
How you disguise this reality is your blatant confusion
For what you spend your life seeking is just an illusion
~E.S.P.

sad clowns

Clowns should never fall in love.
Love is depressing.
And sad clowns aren't funny.
And when a clown isn't funny
they have nothing to live for.
Without anything to live for
clowns play their final joke.
It goes like this:
"Why did the clown blow his brains out?"
To get to the other side.
~I.C.L.

BED of WAR

The room reeks of beer and burnt cigarettes
The sheets are stained with despair and regret
Nameless faces strewn across his bed
Bare bodies rendered lifeless and left for dead

He takes their hearts and sucks them dry
To quench a thirst he would never satisfy
A silent exchange, barely a word spoken
Over too soon or too late, leaving both broken

His smiling features are now frown shaped and rigid
His loving heart has long since gone frigid
His hardened qualities only draw them in
To spend a night filled with lust with sin

To think one person could transform him to this
A villain that could break hearts with a kiss
He would spend his days searching for love to burn
Like the one he gave his girl, which she didn't return

There would be another girl coming soon, and she wasn't the last
And for a few more hours his heartache would be masked
He would tell her he loved her just to make her stay
Then leave her heartless by the following day
                    ~E.S.P.

I have not seen the light of day
Am I a freak?
Not normal so they hid me amongst the rubble.
Wearing a cloak of invisibility and non-existence.
Pants of shame and self loathing.
When walking the halls people pass right through me.
Writing helps.
This is a culmination of 16 years of bottled up emotion. A
poem of life. In the end, no one claps.
~I.C.L.

metaphor

With a shaking hand I took to paper, using my words like a sword. I weaved you in every line, thinking of every moment, feeling, and regret. I assigned you similes that would infuriate Shakespeare, shot out rhymes fueled with pain, and documented us in word play that rolls off the tongue. In time, you no longer became the main idea. I could no longer write about instances I could not recall, conversations I had gone lengths to forget, and a touch that would now be foreign to me. As you faded to black I dropped my pen and thought maybe your eyes don't quite sparkle like the Sun.

I am a memory and our love is just a metaphor.
      ~E.S.P.

unknown love

She thinks she is crushing
Hard.
She goes through the day
thinking of him.
Thinking of when he will notice
the tears on her face
and wipe them.
Others call her,
text her,
want her.
She only needs him
and he only needs
to open his eyes.
~I.C.L.

rest(ing) with peace

"You know what?" she snaps, jumping up from the couch with her fists balled. "I just can't do this anymore."

"Fine," he shrugs. She hesitates, then shakes her head in resignation as she grabs her stuff.

"Wait," he says with her foot out the door, a last minute protest she was just starting to think would never come. A smile almost plays at her lips as she turns to him.

"Don't leave me," he says, his face low to hers just how she likes it. "Please."

Just as his lips brush against hers the vision fades to the black darkness of her bedroom. It's ten minutes later from when she last checked the time. Only an hour before her morning alarm. The room is still empty, she's still alone, and he's not trying any harder.

She flips her pillow on its cooler side and searches for sleep and solace. Hoping that somehow, somewhere, there is serenity.

~E.S.P.

inner solace

The rain beats down
Like a torrent of notes in a concerto.
It beats down my face.
I looked at my feet to remember.
Remember why I took this melancholy jaunt.
To remember what went wrong.
It started when I retired
And ended when she left.
The in-betweens are nonexistent in my mind.
As I returned home my keyhole seemed different.
It seemed I could not fit my key in my life anymore.
When I walked in I went to the cabinet to get some Oreos.
The milk I needed was iffy because the label
Says it expired weeks ago.
I guess I didn't notice it slipping away.
As I bit into the calming chocolate and cream I realized.
This girl made me lose myself.
She took a part my bearings on life, and my emotions with her.
And she's never coming back.
Out of the silence in the corner of my eye
I noticed a moth emerging from its cocoon
And noticed I was okay.
~I.C.L

babygirl

"I don't know," she says to me. "Sometimes I just don't see the point anymore."

She says this with her eyes downcast and her arms hanging by her sides limp and lifeless like she's already dead. Her hand twitches before she turns the ring on her finger around, something she always does when she's nervous. She glances up at me because she thinks she's said too much and she wants me to throw her a life preserver, an okay that it's okay to not want to be here sometimes.

She's physically weak, her zest for life is gone. She no longer believes in fairytales. She's too afraid to announce when she's unhappy and doesn't trust anyone who thinks she's beautiful. Her desire to scrutinize the earth has diminished to the want of one, *just one* stress free day and I think it's sad that she no longer demands what I consider basic human rights.

Once upon a time she was a little girl who sometimes played with Barbies and other times with dirt. She could create stories like a seasoned educator, made every walk a voyage, and smiled at strangers because it never crossed her mind that anyone could hurt her. This little girl called herself princess, and it was okay that no one did because she knew in her heart that she was nothing less than royalty.

That little girl has not left. She is waiting somewhere deep inside her, deep inside me, deep inside all of us. She's smiling even though her front teeth are missing, but she doesn't give a damn about how she looks. She has a baby doll and a teacup in her hands and wants to know if you'd like to play. She wants to know why you don't call yourself princess anymore.

I see that little girl waiting for you. Set her free.

You are free.

~E.S.P.

Troubled Minds

You say I can tell you anything, but how can I express
The craving I have for your head on my chest
The yearn for skin I have barely touched
Just an "accidental" brush before I become too much

I'm sick of love poems, I'm sick of emotion
We can't stomach peace so settled for commotion
Is my smile too fake? Is my laugh too loud?
I'd like to start this poem over if that's allowed

Troubled Minds

You say I can tell you anything but how can I express
The emotions I fear are too deep to confess
I fear an awkward smile or worse, a fake laugh
Let me start over 'cause this is a really rough draft

Troubled Minds

You say I can tell you anything but how can I express
How can I confess, how can I get this off my chest?
I don't want to be different, lord I don't wanna be
Another forgotten grain of sand drifting off to sea
Can I have your company, can we stay up all night?
Can you hold me close and make it alright?
Can we laugh, can we cry, tell me what can I say
To convince you to be here when dusk turns to day?
Do you think of me when your mind can't find sleep?
Are you scared that you too have fallen too deep?
Do you like to party or prefer staying in?
Do you want to take me to the fun places you've been?
Do you replay our conversations over in your head?
Do you picture my body heat warming your bed?
Do you eat your Oreos raw, or dip them in milk?
Can you settle for cotton or only accept silk?

39

Do you kick yourself when you don't get an A plus?
Does your head bang against the window when you sleep on the bus?
Does your mom blow her top when you come home past three?
When you hear the word "love" do you think of me?

When you say, "you can tell me anything" you need to know
How deep and troubled my thoughts could go
You're always in my head, you sprint through my mind
Let's just start over. I'll get it right this time.
~E.S.P.

so yeah, I guess we're all a little bit troubled ¯_(ツ)_/¯

www.ingramcontent.com/pod-product-compliance
Lightning Source LLC
Chambersburg PA
CBHW071748020426
42331CB00008B/2226